LIT

Ron Silliman

for Edith Jarolim
Being a part of The Alphabet

Potes & Poets Press Inc. Elmwood, Connecticut. 1987

ACKNOWLEDGEMENT

Magazines are an essential link in the community of writing. Portions of this poem have been accepted for publication in *Bluefish, The Difficulties, Fiction International, Five Fingers Poetry, Modern Times, Pavement, QU, Sapiens, Sink* and *Tramen.* I want to thank the editors for their support of my work. Special thanks go to Tom Beckett for his extraordinary support, and to the National Endowment for the Arts for a Creative Writing Fellowship which enabled me to devote time to this work.

cover design: Richard Wilkins.

ISBN 0-937013-18-8

I

Blue.

Lube.

Big. Boy.

Then. Theme. On time.

Saids. Bide. Buddy. Up over. To bending pony.

Clued. Sod. Winnow. A million. Rerecords records. As if into the Saturdays.

Sloop. Lien. Armor. Samantha's. After the ballgame. Utilitarianistic. Pronominal Andrewsiana (s)talks without.

Widths. Sheik. Any. 3 legged. Bone dry tone deaf Tim. Grounding into Pepto-Bismol. Between taking the winter ballast by streams or knobs. More pods of brass weather rotate into plates of ungoverned nearness within the blank(s).

Thames. Tens. Pass tense. Sincerely. Blue glass of syntax. It nearly forms the figure 8. He nearly forms the figured gate, but then he doesn't. Within, between, but then again, protocol's minuet, series of minute glances. The dance, as you relate it to the rabbit, is composed of chance operations the shape of an hour glassed in a hand-captured liquid.

Good. Dong. Needing. Double parks. Pigeon's 'jammys' cuff. Telephonic necessities. Nicety's not so hot in a nutshell (in the bag). The further raja's foregone pleasures deteriorate, the finer the Spanish shot. Cat's dream smiling mode of landscape decor, rotary at the hypotenuse, oblong twitch, (your verb here) the batons, analgesic and blue. Cod's reams filing index to the stars against class kind of begonia-odored apertif full of views almost introspective, twilight hinged with neon, crayola at the dusk so very wicker, vowel blend or Melitta.

Stems. Tends. Within. As any. Schizo-affective. But the birdshit, it all coheres. Sad as the dragon's fiscal year garden is my bell. Who could have imagined January's smog-ridden tale, whose wagging plot evokes yams? Further arrogance torques the harmonic chemise, no left turn, saran sarong, the gloomy fedora clucking for lack of a green card's vow. Tattoo ducktails (entire stock must go) rivet the ferny glade's ionic duplicates, hand-sewn or virginal as a Chinese jacket, to the tonsarial rhodochrosite splendor, capital M, marketing vacation nights. New model of transfer point sarcasm between aspects of aerial geology autism and neo-heliocentric gestalt, 3 ring punch, hollow shallow pillow, a bird in the sandwich, a dog in the rocker, my hair fading like a morning shadow, is more than you can sip through that straw in your nose, the carbon overdue and those chimes bleating.

Bid. Paid. Aubade. Bitterly. Noncircumstantial. Neo-, not solder, Budweiser. Circus tents all a foam in the garden of light sleep. Cup drinks boy before aghast audience of organization flow charts in a heap. Nose of rhyme's powder clots silver bell of head, berry bush or melon, collies of the green hour bruised, colleagues of the branch, watery & dumb. Aluminum train of fractions sweeps across bitter horizon deep in kaleidoscope at seashore museum according to droll tale passed down from cobbler to mason with fish breaded and wrapped in old news foretelling rain. Before which, detached as Osip Brik and seemingly promoted where the long eros out of acrylic glimmers, liquid pearl at tip of quill, slice of pear in sea of gorp, not anchored to any peer group, mocking as the gull's squawk, the chalk across the green slate as the hall's bell suggests release from arched brow's furrowed irony, finger to the side of nose, the cat sighs. Sincerely and feigning cramps or squinting whispers like any mathematician in jumpsuit and chaps, the aquarium smoldering and hard to digest, cactus in the blender, snail on the glass (in slices) (in spices), in spite of new jaw found deep in Ethiopian dig, an old garage or toolchest as bronchial as my drill to rote version of sky (wrote vision of thigh so soft where the hair starts, curling in the rain-forest tho filled with lice), your eyes attach to rear of head above spine, a stalk whose roots are fond of socks and sex and 6 inches of lox atop bagel's balance sheet.

II

Bead it.

Throngs lean aslant.

The barking is set to strings.
Numbers harden.

Green Ford emerges as pump siphons basement.
Fed Workers Face Furloughs.
Or that new math predicts cholo in a hairnet.

Whipped by street sounds or small scale of Central Park Zoo.
Bloom on the phone tree.
Heat's moisture thumbprints window.
Bites lip, bites glass.
Bodega stanza under new management sells time.

Policy as foresaken.
Two heaping scoops vs. inservice growl.
Flatiron or harpy.
I get your drift.
Uphill, these letters combine.
Monuments of wax paper shimmer in tundra air.
Light bings on over elevator.
Viola watermarks all last night.

Police is mistaken.
Hair turns to swamp under hat.
Landscape the projects.
Flirtation or harpo.
Warped sense of tuber.

Begets transfer.
And then bit down on the chops.
Flowerpot atop gas pump.
Whistler on the trolley.
Swabs of cloud coil off coast.
Set to sprung.
Thereby acrylic valley's squared.
Clogs announce person.

Think of phone lines as houses joining hands.
Squint to write that.
Old woman to store in her slippers.
In bathrobe and mustache and stanza.
Pigeons farming gutters.
Like friends at an opening holding breadsticks.
Gunning the engine or index.
Calendar pages in autumn wind.
Sound of mail in distance.
What frost does to the harvest.
Capitals at margin form a windbreak.
Static, like five shades of amber.
Red and green or red or green.
Hour-like.
The smell of new bread.
Derricks in the gulf pierce skin of earth.
Coffee jitters.
Man in the caboose waves back.
Tar heater has its own sound.
More than a dozen.
Or a pear tree.

Guy in back of a firetruck is the tillerman.
Information squeezes brow.
The clown is inflated, weighted at the bottom.
Punk is a petroleum product.

You imagine each car as belonging to its house.
Canary Islands start to sing (sink).
How can you think that.
Old cans of Bud in the gutter have long since been flattened.
But the Marlboro pack is intact.
Econoline (decal of Bugs Bunny).
The design of a feather (foxtail) is proof enough.
But that was before Yalta.
Idaho continues to recede in the mind.
It's hard to remember that these scratches are letters.
Each book awaits the rebirth of pulp.
It's combed that way on purpose.
My fern pushes at the window.
Mexican Marxists mix markets.
Histamine.
Syntax presents illusion of depth (pork stomachs).
Clown returns to upright position.
There you go again.
Like the waltz of connotation.
You like the walls of.
Further research discerns organism (hears the tune).
Can notation teach (orgones in a breadbox).
Runes reach extra innings.
This is denied lawful admission to the World Bank.
Clouds push light from the sky.
A silhouette in the window is engulfed in flame (details at eleven).
Repeats literature without which.
The tubing leads to the anus.
A high-gloss enamel.
Combined in the bowl of an eye.
Adult speech.
Further rabbit.
Expropriate them kulaks.
Garage door seen as margin.
Number, more numb.

Speedball kills obnoxious genius (a habit).
Credo: these drops of rain are not related.
Nor has the Polish General contributed greatly to the fashion of dark glasses.
A gloss polishes a footnote.
Humpback gargles krill.
Timesheets are due.
The evenness of the lawn's a conspiracy.
Such as rectangles in the history of dirt.
Against a white wall (8½ by 11).
Conceived as your breast (in my mouth) so recently returned from the dentist.
An actress sells the cobbler a trout.
The infielder's bicycle is burning.
The marketing subgroup is brainstorming (sheets of butcher paper taped to imitation wood panel.
The hotel is responsible for pastries.
Orgasm is a consequence.
As to nouns lacking objects.
Volcano is the planet's sigh.
My kitty-cat craves chicken.
Pagination is a twitch.
Distinct from deforestation.
Enter amount due.
Place tongue softly just over clitoris.
Fold whites into the batter (a pitchout).
Time for a second cup.
The stillness of old men on a putting green.
Rusted sawblades hang on the wall.
The parrot is blue and yellow.
Which is the insurgent.
Old power mower abandoned under the lemon tree.
Here, too, garbage trucks are red.
And the dog's name is Bruno (a temporary dog).
Silliman is wrong and I can prove it.

Sirens beget collage.
Those little riverbed homes must flood.
More music.
Or the rooster in the distance.
Between thought and action spills the syrup of history (suspiciously red).
Nissan stanza.
Mixed aggregate.
Fleas.
The thoroughness of despair or morning.
Watch how a bird settles on that line.
An old lawn chair in the weeds.
One last red poinsetta.
Chicken of the sea.
Deficit writing (the word is its function).
Masturbation is so tender.
The sky (described) is sky blue.
Or the colony of flies in the shade of the porch.

The task of sleep.
Generates the chorus of birds against the distant percussion of a pile driver.
America in love with its space truck.
The intersection as form (the mailbox).
Deny it.
The elegance of powerlines and high antennas.
The kettle rattles when it ought to whistle.
Hair will dry slowly.
Ravaged by drainpipes.
The potato understood as a bubble.
Not the senses, Rimbaud: disorder the sentences.
Tools in the rain will rust.
The rooster's yodel answered.
drive, he sd
The potato understated as a bauble.

The descent of the 727 (deafens).
What is a group but a series of dialogs (who's "in touch").
What does not change is the will to drink (in a straight line).
Demands on the reader (the bank).
Layered as the forest floor.
Here comes an earwig.
The taller buildings were simplified faces.
Put the word breast in my mouth.
That chair was brown before it was green.
Butterflies as thick as snow.
The whine of a drill.
Late harvest means sweeter (estate bottled).
The voice of a young boy.
The carafe of attitude rings.
80 papers.
Logjam in left nostril.
Conch of an ear.
(At a convention).
The head both glazed and pocked.
Cat plays screen door like a harp.
Deep in parrot laughter.
Kafka considers marriage (or coffee).
Rag mop lap dog.
Kills bugs dead.
Straight from the heart (60' 6").
A towering internal sinister laugh breaks bread alone in a cafe.
Symmetric, like a tear on your cheek (requires stitches).
An old woman taps the window and calls your name.
Pretend that it's not Europe.
Sad, like the imagination of #.
Parallel, linked.
Like the truck in the weeds or the broken boat.
The smallest airplane taxis beneath a 747.
The prostitute has her work.
The appropriate tool for editing is a rake.

Possibly weather is a trick.
Eye contact with a baboon.
Old plastic gallons of milk.
The saxaphone a pen.
Or the noise of clouds.
God is a beast.
We are stuttering the history of windows, stoves.
Small metal awnings.
My regrets to the leaves.
Something alerts the shepherd.
Cuticles & bananas (the herstory of foam).
What are they thinking when they sit alone on their porches in the
    humid dark.
Stamps will argue perforation.
The sunflower is bent.
Big sneeze, wet and noisy.
Just as suddenly, the water pressure returns.
These are the Santa Anas.
Proceed to the next sentence (collect $200).
The fly pauses to watch me write.
To listen to the radio is an acquired skill.
So ugly, so awkward.
Academics are not wrong to fear the poets.
Poodle is generic atrocity.
Lap, generic chair.
This bandage is too tight.
Too apt to rain.
The telephone stops ringing before you can reach it.
The weatherman (laughing) in a bow tie.
Beetle's despair goes unexpressed.
Knight to King five.
A long walk uphill with a large bag of groceries.
Here the computer starts to sing.
The air itself is like to burn.
Muttering in the forest.

Just because the ink is blue.
Or the glassed-in cafes of the Upper West Side.
Snapped together all subtle like.
From west to east the way you read a book.
Saxophone mocks a goose.

Syndromes passed us by.
Tractatus Logico-Philosophicus in a game of charades.
No quality control whatsoever.
The sky reduced to corridors.
Footsteps upstairs (over our heads).
Cereal lodged between teeth.
Huge pores crater the nostril.
Half moon rising on a thumbnail.
Which function we have assigned to the earlobe (the knee).
I stare at the paper, awaiting instructions.
Thongs relearn as lamp.
Old sprinkler head left on a sawhorse.
What the machine can't know is confidence.
As parrot is my witness.
Eligible for 26 weeks with no extensions.
Wine robbed his face of all definition (its eyes like sores).
As tho stanza were a rib cage.
Two rooms and a deck.
A great plate of sky.
Fresh shaved neck.
Dry as checkered fate is.
Ladies, step right this way.
Floss.
(Meaning string or Mrs. Williams.)
Furthermore (this term is redundant).
The long putt falls shorts.
Milk crates in the back yard.
Nor the crocus by the fountain.
Flying bugs the size of sun motes against the heat of the lemon tree.

Vote early, vote often.
No device more powerful than a hinge.
Her see-thru blouse with its coy pockets.
Wide mouth brown bottle of Old Peculier.
Stet.
Or the constant hum of the hot tub.
You know it's important because it's a list.
Urgent is another word.
The wind chimes acknowledge fate.
All the charm of the cockroach (in blossom).
Nearly tips the chair.
You long for a line break.
A bee the size of a cat.
Or the dog with an egg (fat & glassy).
Hoops index jazz kinetics.
Look, mama, no over parade of queens radiates such thrills.
Under very wet xylophones you zip.
NAM into DSOC yields DSA.
An old guy with a moustache.
Rent (as a verb).
The war of tokens.
In need of an outlet for the instinct to share.
By ear, he sd.
(Attached to the head (chained to the bed)).
Are sweet exchanges.
All that aside!
I hate collage.
A false ring (a wrong number) loose on her finger.
Little plastic pots for plants.
Cinderblock.
A spread for the bread, for the bed.
Rug on the porch has gone to pieces.
Old icecream truck is music box on wheels.
Sarcastic mode of flirtation.
Unsigned W-4.

The promise of closure postponed.
Legal warning on milkcrate.
Or having to ride the trolley backwards.
The form of a trailer park is one-storiedness.
Big frond.
Old jeep in weeds is used as lawn chair.
Someone around that corner is kicking a cardboard box.
Re-up.
Frequent stops.
At a party I'm accused of wearing a tie.
Postcard to ex-wife.
Liquids and frictives.
Clear percussive ring of baseball bat dropped atop concrete.
Cat lunges at butterfly.
Lamb thaw.
Persian blue.
Jet streak across lone cloud, minimal design.
Preposition's degenerate verb.
Squid cutlet too crisp.
Dopers in the plaza.
Bus up to campus.
Good head, delicate bouquet.
Count the Harleys.
Narrative thread.
Form crust (children's voices).
Fulltimers savor lunch.
Yeats in despair.
Thru the trees, you never see more than the corner of that house.
Based in fact (breaded).
Pelicans on the water.
The calculus of twilight, shimmering, in the corridors of Sears.
Settling.
Those orange trash bags belong to the city.
Luke Skywalker, meet David Antin.
A chance construction.

On the road to employment.
Decompensates (on the borderline), clearing one's throat.
The rooster.
From which you are cut and placed on waivers.
Seeking plasma.
Out of print.
But in collusion.
A view of the mesa and geometry of new towns.
4 houses on Boardwalk.
Who'd've.
Thought the Navy was so full of boys.
Aerosol and climbing.
The Marias offering Spearmint.
Stripes painted on the donkey.
Branch bending.
On reserve.
Sex perceived as sharing.
The rose stem.
A new line.
The white jeep.
Sky King.
Just because I prefer the Malvinas.
Such glands.
Little penguin's baritone wail.
Sax perceived as shearing.
Cardigan over plaid.
Old Prussian blue licks a paw.
Chew a torta.
Canned soda, Tecate in a bottle.
By the numbers.
Thus a garden.
As if the tide.
Farts of the city.
Sox perceived as a shaving.
Six received as a halving.

Or have not.
Vats of experience.
So what is a person.
But a stanza.
Arbitrary and intimate (arbitrated and ultimate (are berated and
estimate)).
Parental guidance advised.
Prenatal, disguised (and gusted).
San semilla.
Web visible because it reflects the sun.
But to a guest, sponges look alike.

III

Hoagy's busted in San
Salvador & B's skull, bulblike, glows
conspicuous in the hardened dark, hot
tub on a hoist, big jets bloated and wobbling
in a final descent, surface smeared in a syrup of strawbs
or the perpetual fear of genre, the slim cat brown
but with blue eyes, what the night
does to these birds these windows
that your teacher so desired, giggling
with ignorance, a lower card of the same suit but
with two eyes and the hands reversed (thumbs up), holding
a cup from which to sip, such
engines in the distance suggest new maneuvers as the band
tunes to perform a cover, a bee
yellow as the alphabet and as hard
to start over or the primates full of sugar and
sweating in the peach-light by a T-square as tho
these straps about your chest
being tightened led to rhyme, thieves
trapped in the traffic with no choice but to go
a.m., or edit the procedures, the flaking
in the eye and smell of yoghurt is to the parrot's
cautious answer that the phone lines or
propellors forgot to gargle or make of this as
recursive a season to days of the weak and willing
to get on, a new dog but temporary
by which to ascribe the sky
through counting, one box for names
but then what is a garden but
tissue at the bottom which once wrapped shoes
all vowel-like and messy with pride in your nipples
reduced to function in the patio's glare and

whiff of burgers diagrams the diver's splash by
the lawn chair and vice and secretary-treasurer
still to be determined with a signature on
the outside where Pookie's in
the foxtails watching a monarch
comment on the Falklands, those hang-gliders out over
the cliffs (motionless, red-yellow) do not
signify an emotion expressible only in sighs, beach blanket or
tetherball, the sequence of yards each the assertion of
a different grass while the porches are settling
comic or sad, visited by the young postwoman in
government shorts, that cocoa butter smell to the
beaches, air full
of radio and frisbee, battleship convoy
anchored at the horizon where the inevitability of sunset's
brilliances discounts the morning silence shaped
by birds not visible in the shade of banana trees until
a telephone rings and you step inside
to discover that it must be
some other house, yellow or green or
mint, the little cuplike wrappers dark brown
and pathetic in their emptiness, an afternoon as
long as California, with sprinklers and a small ache
in the lower back when lifting
the dark blue crates of distilled water
twice a week against the music box tune of the ice cream
truck or the claim
that the suburbs were a true past even
to the caesura, the glance, a stuccoed chimney or
the tone of a garbagecan dragged
up steps the new hire, nervous and
polite, shoes shining, his loosened tie
a careful study like knowing
just how far to bend over
at the water fountain or the proper

tone to the pilot light is not
a solution for aphids, the cat in
the jeep in the weeds, peaches
big as a walnut, cement truck
with a bell for backing up, something
to put on your resume or swallow q.i.d. for colors
brighter than bright and expensed, tenured
as an idea or emotion and so in step with
the tunes, bases loaded, twilight thick
with acrylics topped with granola, willow said to be
"weeping" or on appeal, salt crust rings
the rim of the glass and you recall
what you'd set out to do, mornings lost
waiting for the coffee to hit or
two weeks of wildflowers in the Anza-
Borrego and Mr. Johnson
is able to see you now, but down
the corridor a boa sleeps on the xerox,
coiled and shitlike and a new jet
departs every seven minutes, Balinese
term for monkey, Associate Monkey or
Full, this statement is false, mood elevator
at the zoo, day of no mail if this line is being
remodeled is to the hummingbird
sufficient cause so that your ears pop
and then the knuckles, the pattern
of an old foundation on a vacant lot, jello amid lettuce, the cat
knows to get off the table versus
a spider in the tub, a knot
in the gut compounds
the sentence (fracture), coffee cans
used as planters and all the laces
looped (blue lube, big boy) into center until
you get it, are with it, butterflies
by the mulch trying to avoid that second

transfer unless to an express
meaning, very little units, like knowing
the inventor of the ball typewriter likewise
developed Tang, registered connotation, a tint
of real anger filters all, one jar
for gefüllte fish, one
for ceviche as though guilt
by association to the next syllable being
next were any more subtle than your own spousal
rape because "it's easier," the bear deranged
begs for nuts and bananas at the main gate flap
in the late afternoon or siecle as the little orange cars
of the skylift float
toward evening at the harbor & the sound
of drinks and weren't those flamingoes something, a code three
in the distance only requires
that you raise the volume, the reports
are due quarterly and for this
we ask what is
a line and who cares for their feathers now, a fog
that burns off but sets the tone
to the whole day, not enough
imitation mayonnaise or the bulb
in the bathroom's blown, how can you
watch the orange cat spray
all over the University of Pittsburgh Press, dramatic
monologue of a false self, a bloop
single or the run
in your stocking, nothing is
grounded and enjambment smears or
sneers, the old power mower
rusting away, a dull spring in the long
season which like the horsehide
is loaded up, but the parrot screams
in his cage all day long, yellow

and blue, the pilot
lights up the big jet onto the runway, the guys
at the roominghouse live on its steps and
someone's been sleeping in the park, that
vomit's dried to the sidewalk, & through
the open door you see
the television running
though the room is empty.

IV

We know who they are, beards flecked with straw, collars buttoned, blood crust under fingernails, the terrible breath, sideways glances, roughing Derrida up in a Czech jail, signatures in triplicate, salt rings round yellow margaritas, jigsaw puzzle in the lobby of La Valencia Hotel, the too-thick sweaters, rich sunsets, Conan in Manganese in translation (in full view of pelicans), voice found at the piano bar, profuse apologies denying tenure, 3 balls per game. Content-centered, the dog threatens to bite. Mouth closes slowly over friendliest of genitals. Deep in the garden flowers harden. A sea of unread faces, a day on the deck. New metaphor of tone in a bowtie. The fact of the wheelbarrow at the event of a porch. Talking to the notebook as I write. Barbwire about auto row. To the margin. She-males out cruising on Broadway, secretaries in the plaza spooning yoghurt, yellow floaters of the tuna fleet's nets. Ought to row/out to the island.

Further days seek silence (sentence). What are you going to do with all those connections (trash bags of smashed cans)? So she lives with her shopping cart and small dog in a doorway. The blue parrot does not refer to Casablanca ("red dog, red cloud"). A partial clearing would be grounds for a party. Bottle of Night Train juts from his pocket. The heat of the coffee thrills my teeth. Urine Plaza. The compost is steaming, filled with allusion. Or that Stendahl = Michael Gottlieb. The loud crowd chanting "Rupe, Rupe!" The parrot is no swan.

Oriole gorging on the peaches. Nor was father apparent (seek senses). Grammarian asleep under cactus regrets dream. Game cartridge to flamingo full of shrimp: the renewed native barbarian naturalist checks notes to corroborate syllogistic activity (Celsius). Mountain comes to rest on a shot glass. Even the jeep needs time to focus, arms wet & pink climbing out of the side of the pool. 44 board feet at three turns per year. Ten centuries of civilization caps a tooth (cellophane tape on a school). People with two first names. The B side is slower, subject to fits. Limo glides to depiction, enough butterflies to darken the sky. The chairs are having chairs again.

Only realism can boil an egg. Asyndeton than sinned against (seeds salsa). An old man and his dachshund. The problem of givebacks. The slow gait of a camel (its beautiful eyes). Weaves a world (weave me alone). Paragraphic. Autoredact. Try walking away from a good thing without a sense of disaster. They import water from over the border, long lashes, new abstracts. Noonish (Was ist ein Satz?). A short walk from the sea.

Interruption generates summer, supper (an RV on a suburban lawn with the sign "Your tarot read here"). The androgynous economist trademarks lips and tongue. New theory of twilight. After nachos comes sex. Or that Noland is Frankenthaler made neat. The blue parrot jealous of the simplest finch. I still haven't mentioned oranges. Boxes and brigands. Over the overpass to old Pot Hill. An emotion midway between anger and despair. The usual crowd at Taco Palace. The parked cabbie fast asleep.

Take your prolixin. Everything is syntax (there is no meaning apart from the world). Cats are not children. The old Coke dispenser in the weeds forms a better toolchest. Your mother's image is indelible, reflected in the soup. Machines vend lies. The window is not your friend. The ocean was intended. The image reverts to pink and green. This is a narrative (you will die). The jet sets down in the desert. The sun streams into the sea.

Slower and more elaborate, intentional because I want it, aware of all these birds, the screaming in the trees fused with song, the ice cream truck and the rooster, the many cats, the young man in the next yard who speaks no English and is dying of cancer: verbs scar. Last night on C Street somebody died. Later there's a party, but your eyes are brown and wide (what few teeth I have are yellow). Let's read the Sunday Times instead at the cafe, sipping cappuccino; you can buy these Chinese diaries anywhere. There once was a time when a French actress would let herself be named Miao-Miao. Minnesota is so hard to imagine. For 12 weeks in San Diego I had packed 200 lbs. of books. The yard spoke of long inattention. The ostrich's hat is cocked. He bought his own robe to wear to commencement, bright red. We gradually pushed the hot tub up the flight of stairs. You either have reservations or you make them.

Later you look back into the glare of a calendar, the stare of a cat. My own penis disappears into those wonderful folds of flesh. The pelicans share that spit of land with the laziest of seals. Noise of the kite. Enclosed please find my resume: lagoon. Airplanes look so stiff. His lawn chair rose to an altitude of 16,000 feet. The plastic flamingo on the wood fence is a wind vane. Thus the merit increase is denied, the bank patrolled by an old man too small for his gun, the freeway nearly empty of traffic. She hops through the water to get to the faucet. A tiger sighs. Gulls struggle to fly against the breeze.

Summer! The hills dry. The wind shaking the ripe plums from the tree. The small kids use a tennis ball to play baseball in the schoolyard. I can barely read my own writing. Not one house on the block owned a dog. Tenses were optional, a flight from emotion. Whose turn was it to do the dishes? They fired birdshot into the exercise yard to force the prisoners back into the cellblock. The smoke from the barbeque was intense. Those who knew better weighted the clotheslines with plastic jugs of water. The only music was a distant hammer.

The blood of your period covers my dick like a thick sauce. There are so many positions and no two chairs alike. We lay exhausted, silent, in one another's arms. A funny sad story about an x-rated motel. Large bowl of nachos. Long strip of beach. Gutters is not New York-specific, nor Mick Jagger on a camel. Every bad small museum in America owns one Rauschenberg. Panties dangling from the tv antenna. I'm alone on my porch with a notebook. The planes depart always in the same direction. The parrot chuckling in his cage.

The mould of institutions shades the thought blue, a scarecrow which attracts birds. The small rug on the step turns grey in the rain. A Kantian inscription of hopelessness learns to count syllables while the peasants of data processing lie drugged in the streets. The smell of ammonia through the open bathroom door. The secretaries run the department. The prairies are soon to be joined by tracts, but the bar itself is crowded so long as on the large screen two black men bleed for our pleasure. Radio demands the commuter and fog settles before sunset. We get a gang of lumpers from the docks and beat him to emeritus. But, in the damp forest shade, mushrooms swell. I don't intend to homogenize my meaning for the sake of an enemy. The directions on the machine at the transfer point are not certain. So we eat pork bows and parchmint chicken in the tea room on Hang Ah Place.

Lit, then flickers, whispers, flashes out. The horned owl sits still in the fir tree. The buckram heart, no better than a C+, deflates. Loss is as fixed as the sea. Blisters bubble up on the balls of one's feet. Ink hardens. Seed sinces. The jay could read my thoughts. Those butterflies taste awful. The rose blooms on the light-table, the fish glows in the dark. The man with his pushbroom crosses the bus depot floor. Three pigs got two bros spread-eagled against stucco wall.

V

1

The city of glass is warped!

Still photos of point of impact.

Money reduced to cinders.

2

Twelve blocks to the nearest cup of coffee.

Sunset brilliant with its poisons.

On the doorstep they speak in French.

3

Under brightly colored tents sleeps a village of campers.

Gusts of low fog dampen your face.

The brown mare with one white eye.

4

The mind itself is simple, fluid.

A museum abstracts the duty of the leach.

A zucchini will assume a shape.

5

Between *a* and *the,* the children of a thousand grocers grow up,
consumed with sadness.

Small boats seek fish at the edge of the storm.

The dice cup slams against the wood of the bar.

6

Each new page insults the past, only to apply for membership.

The school teacher patrols the yard at recess.

A man in a room hits his forehead with the butt of his hand.

7

A tramp steamer pulls into view.

400 soft focus photos of seaweed.

The dog leaps to catch the stick.

8

Bees are harvesting the clover.

The sky remains grey for weeks.

The tricycle lies abandoned by the steps.

9

The militant syntax of the surrealists has begun to froth.

Friends gather in the kitchen.

Old clay pots that await the return of dirt.

10

The sun shines on this sentence!

Enjambment is like a bunt.

The pelican dives beak first into the waves.

11

She lies awake at night, crazed with retiling the downstairs bath.

This line is the trump.

Bulbs of the fuchsia about to burst.

12

The pushcarts of Orchard Street still vend crap.

The meat of the mango is orange.

That one step has been loose for years.

1

The shades are not raised until sunset.

An old clock recasts day in two circles.

The couple is jogging in identical sweatsuits.

2

Nature abhors a dachshund.

The grape tastes sweeter than imagined.

Try writing in a stiff wind.

3

Style in calculus soon curdles.

The basin designed as an altar.

How the toothpaste gets into the tube.

4

Tamed by Milton, I lie on Mother's head.

The bee was a large as a mouse.

The bush grew against the side of the house, huddled against the wind.

5

Slightly left of Macy's.

The banana had gone bruised and squishy.

The beer can on the sidewalk had been crushed flat.

6

Words out of context will eat your face.

They just hang out at the corner store until dinner.

Have you signed your check?

7

All money is emotional.

The skyline of Pittsburgh at sunset.

Add milk.

8

New fee-for-service sought for poetry of cramps.

The third baseman leans into the stands.

Wave pounds into the shore.

9

All these backyards left uncared for!

The thin gold chain about the base of her neck.

The grass all burned off before summer.

10

We sat beneath an umbrella, eating avocados stuffed with calamari.

The Pinto paused at the intersection, ready to make a left turn.

Knight to King's Bishop three.

11

Handbound, the volume is gorgeous, with no hope for an audience.

So she went to the academy to become a beautician.

Administrators *want* to act guilty.

12

Nowadays purges are carried out by computer.

They were deprived of their zipcode.

New suns begin to compete for the sky.

1

Their last hope was to wed the daughter to the landlord.

Wet and obscene, like a grapefruit.

But in the drawer was a small knife.

2

The 3 pigs are aryan, the wolf big and black.

Did he say his name was Al Pesto?

Up pulled Pat Brady in a jeep.

3

Bare arms attacked by the shadow of a bee.

Compound sentence, dependent clause pushed through the flesh.

The flags of three nations oppress the plaza.

4

The simplest thing (a paragraph) has begun to melt.

The house shudders in the turbojet's wake.

The head of a pig as an element of sculpture.

5

The disincentives have begun to bloom.

The President trapped in a stalled elevator at the White House.

The riot squad loosens up, swinging their billy clubs like baseball bats, doing stretches, bends.

6

The people walk with their eyes turned to the sidewalk.

The yoke settles into one half of the shell, the white into the other.

A desire to confront the unimaginable leads to a postcard collection of camels.

7

The unit cost per stanza is a concern to this panel.

But to name your child Donkey Kong?

A bowl of plums alone on the table.

8

Sand blows up from those gray lots.

Teeth lurk behind full lips.

There are two kinds of money: painting (bills), sculpture (coins).

9

The house was cut into flats, so now there's a closet with stairs.

Mom's not looking for a lateral transfer.

The cat plays with the mouse until it stops playing back.

10

This felt less like jail than summer camp.

Jittery with coffee, but wanting to yawn, I close my eyes in the sun.

That tree's capacity for asymmetry is what defeats me.

11

Then a whole generation resented its work

That woman's son is a street person but visits on Sunday.

The small dog was about to be noxious.

12

The lawnchair represents despair.

Red wine kept in the fridge.

The mower at the garage sale caked with rust.

1

The tyranny of the whole molds its parts.

History leads to the t-shirt.

The finch yodels, ignorant as a plum

2

Exaggerate the valley to construct the road.

He imitates famous men, industrial sounds, the shapes of chairs.

Deep in the forest the woodpecker knocks.

3

Fresh asphalt is mushy, ground for Melitta.

Disassemble the bikes of short prose!

All these shingled rooftops on the slope of a hill.

4

At Small Press Traffic, the books are divided by sex: men, women, fiction.

So you move to Rochester and look for a job.

I wait for the mail.

5

Even the string for the bean plant presents an idea.

The bath mat out on the porch to dry.

Your back stairs as seen by a sculptor.

6

Modernism sought to construct a mouse.

Later, we had carbons.

The library open only three days per week.

7

The Dane is crowded into the back of the truck.

Overlooking the cove was an old pink hotel.

Thus ice cream cones should be pointed at the bottom.

8

Everyone looks to see which house the cop car pulls up at.

Response to enjambment is one in ten.

The cane is a permanent addition.

9

The RV in the driveway is his other life.

Big plaster cow above the market's marquee.

In the comp light.

10

The round scar on the table from a hot pan.

Ten rooms in a warehouse of unsold books.

Blue-striped toothpaste.

11

The fix is in.

Due to declining enrollments, dissertations on sci-fi are now permissible.

The old campus would be a good site for an industrial park.

12

Your Wittgenstein as played by Bogart is getting stale.

The fuzz of one peach versus all of Larry Bell.

The pelican on the side of the rock.

VI

The region itself is L-shaped, a string of towns down along the coast, then suburbs spilling eastward to the mountains, beyond which lies the desert. In the spring when the jacaranda blooms, the streets are lined with purple. Those young navy boys don't know a drag queen when they see one. At the base of the bridge is Chicano Park. All of the students wore cutoffs. Melvyn suggests a game of charades. My room was painted seven different shades of white. By now their child had acquired language and was giving commands. Your middle name is Brenda. They went to a spa in the desert where she complained of the lack of books. The Padres or Pads or Pods. I began to listen to the radio for the first time in years, relearning its structure. She was on the executive board of AFSCME. The parrot was blue and yellow. That's where they build the cruise missile. Downtown, the main plaza was half torn up, causing the winos, players and preachers to huddle close together. Many buses stop at dusk. I had not lived alone in a decade. The prose class was very male. I had the high score on the Qix game over at Taco Palace. Down by the fence several large marijuana plants were ready for harvest. I can appreciate the compulsive talker. Their pitcher, Lollar, could hit too. Two doors down, the rooming house slouched in disrepair. I went to the junior college library, looking for a typewriter. He was always bringing home a stove or old cameras, or even a Packard bought at an auction. The crossing at the border is a series of ramps. They spend more time at home now, watching the tube. The tap water tastes horrible and leaves a white coat on all the pots. One thousand birds greet the dawn. I went to the bookstore Geoff's dad had owned, its entrance golden, the result of shelves of National Geographic. After the film we went to a bar and talked. They imagined themselves punk but were modest. A constant stream of landing aircraft. I don't write to teach. She's drunk before noon. I sat at the wicker table on the deck, enveloped in bird noise. Ernest Hahn owns this town. The banks close for siesta. A walk on the beach in the dark. In the park before dawn, you can hear the lions. He wants to play with the poets. With that big blonde grin she said, "I've never experienced guilt in my life." I was jogging four, five miles each day. It was a lesbian-run coffee house, but open to men. The bed was three foam mats which piled into a couch. Antin kept promising to "get together," but never called. Kaprow was silent. The part-timers are the only ones who ever make sense. She tried to sleep with her student, but he was too frightened. His come-on was overwhelming, an inverted shyness. Up at the cove we'd find pelicans. Nowhere else can you get margaritas by the pitcher. I took the manuscript to be xeroxed. The largest porn shop on Fifth Street is in a building owned by the son of President Ford. She tried to fix me up with the law student who lived upstairs. What will you remember most? The little old wino actually lived in that horse trailer parked on the street. This name: Heatherbell Fong. The adolescent narratives were virtually identical, but with men were ironic tales of lost love, and with women stories of sexism and alienation. That's the hotel in Chandler's *Playback.* The museum's view was better than its art. His new wife shook my hand, nearly breaking three fingers. The hoist got the hottub halfway up the stairs, but we had to build a platform to take it up the rest. She spoke matter-of-factly of how, if necessary, she would bury her husband and son. She's blonde and skittish, a good writer, but terribly unread. When we cross that border, penis and vagina, nothing will ever be the same. The film was shot in Beirut. The canyon in the park had been stripped to build a hospital. Everyone has a story about the plane crash. I made her a cup of coffee to sober her up. The entire diningroom table, filled with food and bottles, simply collapsed. His localism was admirable, although a dead end. I never got to the archive. She makes the best flan. The sailors love to bus up to the nude beach. I come over to watch "Hill Street." Her affair with Bob was intense. At the zoo a seal bullies a penguin. I like my coffee so thick it's bitter. We order a bowl of nachos. You can see Mexico from the deck. You were married once, and are an aunt. Kathy was in a mood. The poet decontextualized by his job. The cat's name is Turkey. He let you know that he was a vet. We sat in the dark, drinking beer, while upstairs Reagan and Peter were preparing supper. When the coals went out he started them with a blow torch. The red robe means he went to Harvard. The concussion fucked up her balance. Only one integrated neighborhood in a town of one million. You rolled over and we did it again. Where are my structures? Landing, the planes filled the sky over my house. The siamese sleeps in the bathroom sink. He opened the bottle of Green Rooster. Walking down the street I'm apt to stumble. The piano player at the Turf Club's named Tiny. A gingerbread Victorian in the barrio where they have readings once a month. So we got stuck in the sand in the desert. Tempy was Fergie's 3000th K. My tongue there, where it does the most good. The firetruck parked at the track, while its crew jogged a few miles, one member left to attend the radio in the cab. The spring scandal was who had not been given tenure. The night after his mother died we went to the game. The donkey's stripes are just shoe polish. I flew to San Francisco for the weekend. We were just up the hill from downtown. "Count your sentences," I would say over and over. The Double Happiness is near Jerry's. Large brown eyes with long lashes. On the official campus map, Che Cafe is Coffee Hut. The high desert is different. A web of shopping centers interspersed with industrial parks. A tall bottle of Corona. A small boxlike apartment, one half block from the ocean. Emotionally, we were both much needier than we'd expected. She said she had something to confess. Barrett taught Aaron to fetch. Your mother's livingroom walls are filled with small religious paintings. What if I hadn't met you on the bus? What if Willie McGee hadn't broken Juan Bonilla's wrist? By the junior college was the inevitable Militant Bookstore. The Vietnamese food here is nothing special. At dawn, I'd see men wander out of the park with their sleeping bags. The kitchen window is always open. A small case of rugburn contracted while fucking. The bay thick with military boats. In her notebook were 52 alternatives for one word in her text. Even wearing a dog collar he looked sort of preppy. He'd been a student in her Spanish class ten years before. Pressure had to be kept on the State Department or Hoagy might just disappear. The Vice-Chairman wandered about the department like a large rabbit. She would show up at office-hour and sit there and not say a word. DiPalma's not getting his mail. I missed the last bus and walked three miles home. More than anything, it was solitude. Rupe circled under the high fly. Ivy grew up the base of the palm. The Mexican women took the bus up to their jobs in the homes of La Jolla. On the floor in two dissertation binders were the collected poems of Paul Blackburn. Each campus has its name and this is Motel 6. In the dark we open the champagne and watch the waves.

VII

Literal transfer. Blows about the face and neck. I don't mean to be the plum tree, but to care deeply, where the pus starts. The false soccer ball is large among the boys, their green sky acrylic and the shortfall growing. Somewhere a shower runs. In the white bowl the cereal has gone soggy, but the milk is sweeter. Indian print bedspreads are not adequate curtains. In a double-play this motion is the pivot. The driver makes the old woman step from the curb into the gutter before she can pull herself aboard the bus. How will this look typed? The henna will wash out. The parrot is want to bite. The old vents are rusted. Cinder blocks built one civilization, then fog. A thick sentence is scratched out. Under the ocotillo the scar of an old camp fire forms a perfect circle, against which the pale camouflage of a lizard fails to work. He sits in his dark garage all afternoon every day. This line is for foodstamps. Into the history of miniatures steps an idea. You cannot sweep glass up quietly. The cat offers its belly for a rub. Within the forest the smell of fresh asphalt gives rise to fear. Who left the lights on? A dense mist settles over the small white homes on the hill.

New paragraph: old tricks. Dear squeegee, vend hither. Cloves pierce the orange rind, while out
the dusty window a neighbor stands at his mailbox staring at an envelope, a rooster crows, and in
my daypack is a broken telephone. The wind is full in the sheets on the line and the pages must be cut
apart before you begin writing. The cat sniffs at the sausage. A small red metal ''glass'' in which
toothbrushes and razors are stuffed. Jitterbugging, here we come! The blue one is the creme rinse.
Mike Heath on a pop fly. Floss. 100,000 Indonesian political prisoners have been kept in jail since the coup
17 years ago. Ex-astronaut Seeks Ark. Rock keeps on rollin', thick mountain of demo tapes. Describe
this breeze: little half-warm gusts. Bees hum in the fuchsias. Dog yawn. In the Tenderloin at midnight the streets
are still lively, folks hangin' out in front of their res hotels, the traffic now mostly taxis
and prowl cars, all yellowed by the streetlamps. A contoured sheet of cartoon cats. In tennies. At dawn
she's in the garden, catching snails. White sky. Dry fern. The banana's peel starts to freckle. In the
kitchen two sisters are dancing to the Stones while the calendar on the wall still shows July.

There's a bee on my knee. Spin cycle. Enclosed please find the self-valuable word. A
young Asian man wearing thick glasses watches me write this through the window of the laundromat where
two small boys circle the washers, playing tag. I see the "help wanted" sign in the donut
shop and think twice. You might find anything on the small shelf in a phone booth. The
drink was a deep blue. The jitneys are cramped but quick. By mid-afternoon it's time to give
up on the sun. Nobody's mutter beats Anselm's. My mother still has red hair. Pendleton shirts
become a cholo fad. Hightop tennies. "Say the tone of an afternoon." Between language and thought
stands a cop. The body shop is in the hands of sculptors: their sinewy dogs look vicious with
cropped ears. I work here. The bath mat is always damp. Thus my sentences sing of love. But when
it rains in the summer and the kids are exhibiting "indoor behavior," don't the burritos look thick with
sauce? Designer pocket? Lease with option? An avant-garde is blessed with amnesia. There's enough
life in a single intersection at rush hour to generate tenure by the dozens.

I just came in to get out of the rain, but's a warm day near the margin. The dustpan fits
onto the broom handle and is left in a corner. We bow to the religion of stanzas, totally
oppressed. The dog sleeps in a fenced yard. Cash-on-cash. So pencils are yellow and a hose for the
garden green. Secondary market. How people still rig up their clotheslines. A minor leaguer to be named
Later. Is that the phone? Artbooks. I yield to the gentleman from South Carolina. Once they are
up those big jets fan out in all directions, but today's clouds are thin and smeared, giving
the sky the feel of a ceiling. The rose has begun to wilt. I hold off until you start to come. What are the arcs
of association? White butterfly amid thorns. All the ways in which an ostrich is not a bird. When
the dog wakes the shade has moved. Old web hangs limp, fuzzed string, straight down from the ceiling. Blue
ink repeats the word: an I stares out, surrounded by syntax, by sinus. That's the flying
banana chair. The old shed is pleasantly musty on a warm day, the cactus in its window bearing a red flower,the
plum
tree in the yard throwing shadows through the door. The old parrot gives a squawk.

Words demand mandatory arbitration: drain the lawn. Pulley squeals perfect pitch. Simple declarations: cargo
argot. Grody to the next and carry to the tens place. Wasps are nesting in the mouth
of the drainpipe where winter is unthinkable. Send a blind copy to Region Nine. A host of
flying things no larger than dust above the clover. The limp in Faulkner's predicates. These spiders
are my friends. Coleus branch sprouts roots in a glass of water. Once a dancer, then a weaver. Why
8½ by 11? Pope's couplets are nonetheless prose. Veal, video, Vichy. Through the roses I can see
the old brick seminary on the next hill and the tree tops from the park beyond, while in the valley (hidden)
the distinct sound of a logging truck churns past. Space monsters descend from the top of the screen. Victoria
Principal? Morning sweat (writing after running). These small flowers are blue-purple. On the west slope
you feel a sea breeze. Who said this was non-syntactic? In the shade is an
old school desk, waxed wood, uncarved upon. I found the clay pot broken and the cactus on the floor in
a mound of dirt. Thus every third Fibonacci number is even (use it).

The sea cloud is dark, a brooding storm. The RV is brown with an orange trim. This seat is reserved
for seniors and the disabled. His prose is better skimmed. I'm drinking milk for good. The hummingbird
taunts the cat. Short and therefore not scarred with style. This layout pro brings his own waxer. That
next line is a doosie. The Army recruiting desk at the unemployment office. The lone pink house
amid a row of whites. My ear today hears different. Memories of past lovers not by sight. The
relay from the cutoff man is on the button. That poor fern is baking in the glassed-in porch. Quantity
itself is one mode of tension. Tall and trim, thick straight hair prematurely grey, muscles etched
under a dark t-shirt, baggy black rubber pants held up by yellow suspenders, the fireman hoses off his own
little car in front of the station. Negative termination. Typically, the values of the board of trustees
are in conflict with the needs of the agency's clients. The parrot is there for friendship and show. Aid
to the so-called developing nations is intended to reinforce existing power relations within them. Of 13 tenured professors
twelve are white men. Boycott Coors. The tiger stares through the bars of her cage.

VIII

"Write often, write upon a thousand themes, rather than long at a time, not trying to turn too many feeble somersets in the air—and so come down upon your head at last. Antaeus-like, be not long absent from the ground. Those sentences are good and well discharged which are like so many little resiliencies from the spring floor of our life—a distinct fruit and kernal itself, springing from the *terra firma*. Let there be as many distinct plants as the soil and the light can sustain. Take as many bounds in a day as possible. Sentences uttered with your back to the wall."

Henry David Thoreau
November 12, 1851

IX

Wild gesticulations, wide
receivers. To shade
white page glare
just write. Decal
on shirt front
is suspect. Boots
for to take
big hill now.
Butterfly. Porchrail
is saw horse.
Red thorns on
old rose bush.

Hand trim lawn.
Under these stairs
find cool shadows.
Poor stereo lacks
one speaker. Shape
of word one.
On line sheets
form sails. Boy
shoots with his
cheeks, ricochets whisper.
Goggle. Blue lube,
big bad boy.

Sliver. Allergic to
detergent. Sun in
row of hard to caulk sky
lights. Think about
toilet seat. Elastic
aesthetic governs tenure,

fear. Sad old
comp prof. These
suburban streets never
taught to curve
go right home.

Single sitting, subtle
settling predicts quake.
Insects on neutral
feed. Restart. Pair
of dimes won't
buy paper, three
ring carny. I
is for farce
but mean that.
Brown garbage can
faded steps. Sky
heats dry streets.

X

Late

Light

I stumble, you sing, they lie in the sun. Now here's an in-service on the DSM-III.

When to not make love demands more
Permanent salsa lunch poem
Shifts into higher gear

The ear is wide
and the word is odd
and and inserts its own
hard tonality:
beep beep beep

I sit on a bench on the edge of the park: descriptions of joggers trot past. Three fat flies lunge at the kitchen window and bounce back. A red rose starts to unfold. The glass doorknob is broken and lies on the floor of the shed. Negative campaign in the race for Lieutenant Grammarian. A plume of white smoke from far over the hill. Writing is eyes. I love the way the flocks compute.

Pen half chawed, the rear
door open but the heat
on as the grey cat is to the couch, lawn
mower, rain shower, slower to
his vocables in a purse
'd lip, "ho ho caribou,"
sleep tips heat's absence, wit

wobbles, here I am, sun
sets, terrible pink orange sky
gets dark, gets down, gets
laid back at the ranch
around the table at lunch.

So simple
set
to strings
kept hidden —
mere lower limit
— margins mirror
fixed borders,
fate
to be born into
if to write
to right
thot ecco's —
Is it words
heard in the hollow
chill of morning
real as
this seat is
cold?
To speak,
speak
the line . . .

Look: the rook in the book in the nook was unable to take a hook. I want a poem real as an allusion. The way people bundle up on a chill day. The heat from the coffee enough to steam the kitchen windows. The decorator mugs feeling heavy. Butter melting into the toast. I want a poem real as an illusion. A row of small clay pots on a fence, awaiting plants. A colony of small bugs dances like motes in the sun. In the paper, description curdles and flattens. Patterns of static construct a radio, sending "please remit" toll-free into the skull, a swollen tomato. You want under? Aliens communicate by code: alligator on sport shirt. As for we who love to be astonished, the doorknob is still on the floor. Is it Bob? These nouns crinkle, all yellow and pink. Ling P. Sicat asks for an epilog. An earplug distributes opposite of silence. The antennae of the race have been snapped off by idle youth. Clarinet in a cat fight. Get drunk before you vote. Thus reasons soil. A small girl beckons her kitty. This scene is repeated, intended to charm. In Jonestown, bloated corpses begin to explode in the sun. Thus seasons air. Find the noun. At what moment do you realize that you will always be forced to rent? Her unstated tenacity only becomes evident over time. He starts up conversations with strangers on the bus. These sentences occur in this order. I hate what narrative does to time. The garden's grown into a jungle. The butterfly is orange and black.

Please hold on sudden stops
the steppes of Russia rush
across a split blue screen
screaming locomotive plumes into Munich
Chicago (fat fingers — closeup — drop
nickel into palm for news
Who gets to be Rosebud?
so sad Who gets to
(so said my Cid) be
dead, hand me my head
This at least I read

One in five is lost
so trump the ghost, best
past in the alphabet, bitter
tea, lower case, faces front
as ball is a font
spinning to print which words
harden harping theme, absurd luck

thus to land at Boardwalk's
red hotel (near to Go
so posit verb as noun)
My brother wears the crown

Rich heart, hard stitch, reach
down, each word one thing
covers many, multiplies out, surrounds
clutter of the simplest desk
in town, realtor sells insurance —
drowns, self service station: book
breaks binding, kids leave home
return, look sadder, haunted, stare
over dinner, silent, sticks stalk
almond chicken, shoots, baby corn
stereo choking one thin horn

4th: the count adds up
Dear gem spa, it's 5:15
(aha) what limit to pure
differential clatter (cough) the stuff
of art (thus fart: Life
parts, the river Jordan, marts
of perfect bondage, margins) starts
to get simple: fee fi
phoneme, name it, sit straight
sing "Hail to the Chief,
he's a dirty little thief"

Young and savvy, soft but
savage, to square the root
cherishing procedure, put down these
syllables swollen in the red
corpuscular pressured pump, it said

it says, to the wall
that is turning, paper made,
trust the next, it's this,
the last, it's that, thought
fattens, trapped in the head
abstraction's presence left for dead.

Let's stretch. To write, I sit in the shed
in a storm. She sent
recently her statute of limitations,
"you slime." Plastic yellow bucket
gets my drift. Door slams.
Is the parrot in the rain?
Is the parent the reinforcer
of a painful narcissistic response
say, as men in a porn shop
imagine autonomy in sex? One sits
long at the livingroom table
drafting the twelve page paper
later returned with just a check — Iatrogenic Maladies:
Etiology and Response. Our Friend the Beaver
by Eddie Haskell. Thus gunowners perceive legislation
to prohibit teflon-coated bullets
as a restriction of their freedom
of speech. Mother calls each Sunday
promptly at ten. The couch
is three foam mats
neath an Indian print spread.
The beach is down the street. The text,
if permitted, encodes time
inexactly. Erving Goffman
is dead. Plum leaves
are blown from the tree. A scale
is something I don't want to stand on
like traditon. The next hill

no longer in sight is nonetheless possible
by virtue of memory
if only you sober up. Tenure
is terror. What if *your* kid
is beaten, his lunch money taken from him,
your daughter fails to come home?
Your head stops still
so that I sense your teeth gently
right at the instant
of orgasm. Which things
come together? Imagine language
on display at the zoo. At the bar tonight
people are making choices
but in the lobby of the La Valencia
a 50 year old jigsaw
remains incomplete. Two eyes
are the cause of depth. Strawberry preserves
on zucchini bread. Negative adjectives
outweight their nouns.
Laughter slaughters laughter.
The library from out of space
has no fourth floor, thereby contributing further
to a theory of number, fidelity.
If you don't have something nice to say,
write it down. Rodefer made note
of Levertov's washer not out of disrespect.
but the nuclear movement, if it is to include
the familiar, must confront the problem of One.
Rochelle Silliman. Who said
I was uninterested in fiction? This rain
will live in literature
for weeks. For once
try simple statements. In here
inhabit the head: half

a loaf. In the doorway
Marcie calls for Emma. We sit
at the head of the steps
to the ocean and sip champagne.
The grammarian thinks to rid
the Department
of poets teaching comp.
The sun rises. The sun rises. The sun
rises. But it's the middle of the afternoon
months later and at night.
The sun rises. The International Dateline
breaks. I want a poem real
as an elusion, taped legs pumping
twist out of the block and deep
into the secondary to await the bomb
lighting up thousands
homes roaring in Utah
deafening as the forest, the self.
These are the simples,
salt in the semen,
two strangers in a Navy town
irrationally fond of camels, off-white
walls, first smell of coffee, a small guy
long dead in a cowboy hat, hot
nachos, Mick's lips, being careful
just to walk down the street
O Miss Margaret Jarvis

The song of abstraction cuts glass, difficult standing up in the boat, ear cupped to the wall, the sun rising or setting or both. Complex phenomena are eaten by snails: escalator clause. Small jars of art preserves. The CPM for upscale is higher. It wants more toner, but the light says "brew," sunny December, towels almost still on the line, a pink clover, Lopping Shear (reggae band), the pen gives off a cheesy discharge. How often only one wants to be fucking. Erica's a teen now (possible source of criticism). Deep in the swipe file, quantifiable and blue, are we speaking colors, between houses, jobs. In this simple sentence we share eye contact, but at one remove. Context creates equivalence: you in an examination room at Emergency with a sprained back, the woman in the next one rapidly dying. Coriander. The half-musical clang of pots. Sound is a petroleum product, thought a gas emitted from the skull. The sun causes you to unfold your fist. What are men? I put the penis in my cheek so that I won't gag. Merit increase. The working class rises up only to change the station, one finger deep inside, subtext transfer point. French guys construct a thought. The generic word is "huh." Barry picks me up for lunch. Icy Fist Grips East. At the end of the line, the driver sits alone in his bus, reading the paper, waiting to start his run. Words are not solids. She shooes the dog indoors with a broom. Predicate engineer. Thus the white hair against the dark skin gives that old Philippino cowboy a *look*. Tho the lot is vacant. One sees the remains of a service station. The auditors crowd in. The smell of a Christmas wreath fills the bus. It's dawn and the neighborhood is full of joggers. The large pen jutting from the breast pocket of the old man's coat looks foolish. Try stamping out that cigarette with a hole in your shoe. At first the word *with* meant *against*: fight with, argue with (*con*test, *con*flict). Maniac sonata. Two weeks for Xmas. Too weak from punning. Wittgenstein's Milwaukee. My grandmother's moustache (copper red). The truss on the table by the bed. Let it all hang out. Let it all bang out a rhythm and call this logic. The dance of the line in the hand in the head of the man writing. Let's invoke Vico, let's provoke Duncan. Floppy disk. An image of order with a spinal cyst. Parrot's name is Tito. Rule one: never kill your publisher. That small table in the kitchen was once the only furniture I had. In another corner, mop, broom and hamper. Why the cat likes to sleep in doorways. Some people cannot let go without trashing the other. Today the sun was only a diffuse light in the clouds. Michael and Michael stood in the rain. Eventually any poster tacked to the wall will start to sag. A huge bag of Meow Mix atop the fridge. A large plastic spinner to just dry the veggies. Fresh bacon on a paper towel. A street walker will want to make eye contact. It wasn't that the boiler was broken: it didn't exist. This year's media Christmas tale is 3 year old sex slave returned to her parents. The Cid Corman Tradition. The pot holders were just sort of lying around anywhere they'd been used last. Now the jargon says cognitive deficit. Blue loop, big guy. Pink and white and in between. In a new town you think you see more because you're paying attention. Not rastafarian, Rodeferian. Dear Cheese, don't be blue. I've got Labriola next to Lacan. Words are not silent, even written in a quiet room. Reality is private, charged with crimes. The lights go out in three states. A gray sweater. The wind knocked the construction worker right off of the I beam. They ran the corner store by flashlight, iron gate closed and locked, taking orders and cash and passing goods through the bars. I go in just to keep the office open. The next morning the air's perfectly still. Then comes the blueline, ready for inspection. Great care in simple words. Buffalo Bob moved his lips, so they never showed him on screen when Howdy was speaking. The light at the end of the pencil (shadows on the wall of the notebook). He's upset that the increases aren't retroactive to the Fall Quarter. The day after, people buy every candle in the state. The cat climbs on the couch. The Giants are a monument to the limits of the imagination. The plum tree is barren, a web of dry branches. Why not declaratives? Time to transplant. You can hear the metal in the oven cooling. Porch light. The tree demonstrates asymmetrical balance. Wait, I thought you were the Other (here at home). Sad fern. The screws on those cheap plastic hooks won't hold in old wood well. Poem lacking unity (pour M. Jacob). Two rings around the moon, one narrow, one wide. Stations of the crass. Rabbits cannot remember pain for more than 60 seconds. These straight lines are a yoke I cannot escape. Fever model. Headset. In France the noun is something different altogether. Two young cats play a sort of tag out in the back yard. The grammarian's handkerchief, his cape. Donor Life. To shape to shock once awake in stock and out, out. What was that sentence? Think of form as a sister, cousins, several people eating waffles, fig jam, game played with pegs on a board with holes. In the bathroom the plaster has crumbled. I will never marry a fat man. That jar has been on the floor for weeks. Your resume shall be kept on file for a period of six months. The sod mister. Twelves. Different values get asserted here. Add flour: the plot thickens. New Xmas jogging gear. At dawn the old men stand outside the Cherokee Lounge, waiting for the bar to open. The name of that place is Wash & Dry Coin-Op. Coda, cola. The accountant shows up in purple coordinates. The neon signs burn all night. The cat goes up the steps in a manner you would describe as guilty. The purpose of a sports columnist is to express viciousness toward coaches. What does it mean, personally, to become a paragraph? I'll have the chimchanga. The diver seen as paused, half within the water. The calendar you get from the corner druggist. The pen as a razor, cutting silence. I get dizzy from too much coffee. What a trowel is for. Known for its fleas. Heat a pot of tea. The shadow of Stein crosses the text. Kellog's Topper, Reggie's Mantle. He liked his few small scars, sensing he had earned them. A blue mold on the spine of *The Cantos.* You go into a coma and choke in your sleep. A typeface would betray you. The chill in the shed is merely physical. This was many years ago. We were far away.

XI

Painter's reconstruction of the color white
Clatter of birds' wings crowds the sky
Sighing, declarative sentence makes wrong judgment or none
Sandwich wrap harbors dark nine grain bread
Out the window, fog shuts sky
Rhyme invoked scandal greases new semi-gloss wall
Head in lap speaks with frozen jowl
Lack of yogurt now seen as misplaced caution
Rolls of roofing felt dot concrete yard
Signing, a straight line stifles cough
New hope for pronouns refunded once again
Pink shape of future lit behind frosted glass

Hint of rain renews odor of lemon rind
Renaissance of moth is hardened, blue heart
Foot encased in wool, then leather
Swami firemen climb into smoke ridden sky
My book, my bowl, old grammarian slouches in
That's why new physics emits false sun
Stationary cloud growing darker and more dense
Sis writes Ecstatic unrelated on forehead
Dead leaves silent to plum tree's horror
Old pipes start to strangle the white basin
Big sigh, the way the walls breathe
Big dream face wants to gel

So noon is self-enforced myth
The status of adjectives tends to cringe
Surrounded, the not high porch offers an inadequate vista
Sex as an idea penetrates an army
No verb will denounce a bias
A statue of mother filling the harbor

Then seven repeats the still bad concept
Automatic cartridge return rising high over U.N. Plaza
The lack of light is its name
Sound certain, sound silly, sound off
Red rover, wind in the clover, over
Sailor boy pays to dance with naked lady

Cat gut, rain is its own rupture, rapture
Brain's a hardened cream of mushroom soup
Insert jellied finger deep into anus
Insist "What a good boy am I"
Two armed duck hunters enter the stock exchange
Ardent aliens harden in coat of light
A cat sits, dreaming in its juices
Stoop opens onto shouting in Tagalog
Electronic transfer of whisper or rice cake
It wants to snooze is a bad sign
Curved window reflects sad flock of goose
Forest of vast moss over spider

6-sided house (or seven) falls down
Neon bosom glow is drink my scotch
Rhythm of evasion at program directors' monthly meet
Bite down hard to discover soft penis
Sun rising in pink dawn sky
Coroner's crew unfolds a dark trash bag
Six legged horse, or 7, kneels down
Sausage seals gold deposit is military regime unstable
Dense cloud swarm threatens memory of stanza
Who are you now, little man
Ridge Road rigid load on hell week
An 8-legged hoss swims in dark water

Slant shingle rooves shelter back porches on stilts
Up the canal by speedboat for crackers

Six cities choke on eraser dust
The scientist's beautiful daughter understands his evil
The clear-headed clean-shaven blond young reporter is single
The herd of wooly spiders crossing moss
Fresh hot coffee drips from its filter
The plum tree pink with spring
The new erudition in subway car graffiti
Faded map with foreign countries in wrong colors
Slow rhythm of lone basketball against concrete
Saucer becomes ashtray for old cigar

Gull gang patrols dull urban lake
Too tall antenna on a lone house
One parrot up against the theory of birds
Cost per tea bag equals one noun
Espousing freely into air bag (sic)
Makes too headed a motion rhyme rhyme
That your jackets possess lining, compromise lunch
The watchband cutting into the fat man's wrist
Edit an idea, change channels, insert dime
Assert thyme, ascertain lime's way, limp
Here kitty kitty where shitbrains still govern
Wax melting where the binding nears the sun

Off-white, a narrow sky begins to close in
Soft hyphens fade against the green screen
Half-hidden, nonremarks curtail attributes, crop predicates
Tough blue Stanza Z-80 shuts engine off
Laugh at a chip shot, the long putt
Often unremembered, the face in the mirror
Coughing fears margin & a second cup
After the tap in, insert flag
Overt horizon, slope now to greet fashion
Rough bumps along the road to break line
Suffer motivation, bright red flare of nostril

Draft image, through which seek shadow

Notes crinkle old syntax's loose sway
Rope bridge in monsoon to far noun
Loom foreign to swampgrass curried in hot sauce
Thus Senator Borah says to another bore
Baby corn, button mushroom, bullet vote
Love it or live it, Dear Barrett
It's 5:15 a.m., that world is over
But I just want Yaz to go forever
Two minutes warning, four minutes to midnight
Half seven, digits on the readout
Count pulse, court passing sums, again Sam
An old broom standing proud in one corner

New nouns for old, no noons for ought
Caffein multiplies the thought into red image
The plum tree is snowing petals
The tall porch landing was her stage
Waiting to load transient program, dog bites parrot
For a general, Ike was so femme
The formalist variation on a double play
Sends Europe south into North Africa
Where to punctuate was mother's next question
Get Out The Vote, capital of South Dakota
Dog bites paragraph parachutes over moldy buckram
Sun disk accesses into driven sky

A broken old pen scratched this
Big wooly spider climbs the stoop step
Months of steady rain silences an urban populace
I squint right at the phosphor screen
Now the sun at the margin
To have what are called good hands
The car backfires and the valley echoes

Depositing ink in swirls to code these phonemes
My state of mind is New Hampshire
Light is but the shadow's absence
A fresh cadence marks a new crime
The lines upon paper state the social contract

Blue parrot sips slowly from an amaretto glass
Jigsaw puzzle down to last dozen pieces
The grammarian's palm begins to bleed
House full of bad pens, bad puns
One year ago tomorrow I went down south
Symbols quest for an impossible full morning
A clerk hosing down the produce shelf
Cabbie's view through the interior mirror
Static, like a postcard from your childhood
Too yellow, too green, the pinks too bright,
To mean anything, to mourn anything, two
People terrified to speak of love

XII

Words wiggle, tickle, setting cat's whiskery nostrils atwitch, rooster's yodel, breeze in tall grass (little spider), grasses, is as/was is (fuzzy), a blue prick bleeds & what remains (flock of gulls) means, O new Spring (!), rhythm is its own plagiarism, doo wop, vowel's valence splitting the dipthong and beneath the kale a thousand snails still in the damp shade, quiet morning, wasp got into the john, bird's call like a gargled whistle, bang, snap, crack, hid in the flowering leaves of the plum, phlegm's but the solids of sleep caught in the throat, the moat, remote, we crossed in the boat, like a bat out of Philly. Folly to count and hope, however fewer, the fix & feel of a clean edge, eye lid, three lies, loafs settle steaming on a hot board (bed), bid 2 Junior Gilliams for a Lew Burdette, get set, said, sad, smell of ripe mulch is sour, our match made of volleys, sulphur, so for how long is that yellow caterpillar set to sit atop hot wet fresh steaming asphalt? Leopards in leotards, hot sauce, spotted cat on the shed roof, blue-gray flicker on the small screen, radios is hard, bad news, how the heat drops when the sun goes, cup of tea, fog tint, hollerin' in the hallway while the desk clerk snores. Later the sun rises but you have to jam the door shut, ear full of wax, car full of vexed doggies yapping in supermarket lot real loud. Lone viking in longboat seeks land across page from crosswords, folded in the old man's lap. Each of many lives seems simple, full of repeats. One job I wouldn't mind losing. After the reading. Referent. Bypass. Bid. Call.

Sought. Sweet. Saw it. Sweat it out. Sad Sultan of Swat. At dusk, the blue-pink horizon. The way you hear sirens deepen when they slow and stop. Swaggering though they don't mean it, a heavy slow grace, the elephants cross the roadway. Head of the snail rears up, horns extended, king of this leaf, leaving its trail glistening, to see the grey jet descend, yard shuddering after. The tongue is thick in the head of lettuce on bread, a lattice said to weave lotus leaves along the wrong path to a single meaning, mining half shades of nuance to mime the world, blue swirl, solid object bigger than a breadbox. Gravity is its own absence nor is balloon racing a sport of the poor, pearls in the sky high over a meadow hover, while below rafters in white water rush, rivers too curl from view, hushed where puppies carry hunters to the fox, boxed in by snapping death, bad breath of a rifle muzzling kin of dog, digs image cut by line from a wood block, inked and then stamped. Thus the blisters of history whisper pus, lives pissed to no higher purpose than poverty's trust in service dense as the surface of a jungle served up under jelly flambe, India my Indiana, say that particulars do not fade nor rust consumed in their own dust, or that memory's fair, an old funeral barely the scene of thought's return, my own father flattened into a photo, false smile no knowing could ever fill, fall becomes autumn but never spring, negative my nugget, if we ever got it, that new syntax equal to the living could just as well lie.

Count friends few just as lovers many, money enters in, plot the poem all lit by reams of writing's trace against the face of one who, were it you, is eye alone at home in the head just as the large bed of the past seduces, the feel of what tongue, wet, widens and hardens what is, just as is wills was its future by being, so a small scar spreads into a canyon from which there is no turning back, only demolition, given that entropy is not perfect rest, even as the debris blossoms each mote of dust bloating into a rotten whole swells so fast that syntax starts to sweat. Hot noon on the sloping steps of an old porch, smell of tar: down in the valley between the tops of trees autos pass, over which the sound of a big truck bearing lumber, but the rustle of wind in the plum branch is louder because more near, I hear the sleeves of shirts slap on the line, all tangled (old white gallon bleach jugs full of water weight nylon, bobbins in the air). Garden orders forest or meadow, the park bares design, clay pot to trap roots, hard edge to the hedge, long rose in a slim vase, knife slicing thru torso of zucchini, steamed carrot growing limp, teeth ripping thru leaf of lettuce, gone. A big cool dumb easy fox gets his index jogged kindly, light moan not of pit quiet roar seeking time under vexed waxy xenon yellow zit. Sun sliced through the bamboo shades illumines the room, one window open to let air in. The sound of pots and forks from back inside the kitchen. The curve hits the outside corner. Upside your fat head. Besides that. Siding. Side. Said.

So. Sad. So soft. So sue me. Lofts in Soho shrink. Rents rise, forcing the poets out. Who remembers the linguist of the Hotel Wentley? White and aimless, cum laude, they have learned which books to purchase, but not which ones to read. The road to Iowa City is paved with good intentions, perfect binding, preferring submission to solicitation, O ragged right. I was not bitter, better, butter being the tiger's fate, finding access where lately excess fought its own fathers to a halt, inhalt, in all the right margins habit sought Rago's white horse, a site for soaring lyric lies. The words are my wife else the mirror break, mere beaked thing worn at the neck, the past is peaked, the page, aging, yellows where black ink hollows out a syntax deep in the stacks of a library not checked out of an infield made of the mind in which spelunkers become fixed by the smell of gas leaking from a pen's tip (tap) along the quay of letters lost, thus thoughts' ruins tossed. Through the print, between the curling graphic spaces, I could see them shitting, grammarians downside up from the rafters in the old hotel, pelicans out over the water, the caged parrot, the Tac Squad in snowshoes at the door, the small girl finishing the ancient puzzle and the distinct fartlike odor of nachos until the salt begins to slide from the rim of the margarita and the weeds in between cracked floorboards start to spell out spring's flowering breach, damp garden of seriphs seen from above understood as a rash thing do, not love but what desire from which I start to sing.

The yard understood as a mixture of motives, porch paint spotting sage and spider, sawdust and old boards killing the lawn, strange bird half yodels in the plum tree against the sound of a garden hose inside a trash can or another bird's higher trill, ears absorb while the eye scans, skin senses the fog's damp, butt upon the step, sound of a broom in which driveway, wind felt in eyebrow's hair, here in the little things (who I am), three flies articulate the sky between porch & tree, poetry is that this thought thus, body but a metaphor (who I was) for a medical model of that thing lit. Of late much work, little light, leads humor stuttering home, get the lead out (of the pencil, the penis), the point scratching paper's skin seen to signify mind means the made marks the maker's mask (meet science), ear stitched to side of head, hard wood weds floor to foot (I am not that), float from word to word as if there were a reason, as if there were reason, beyond *a*s and *e*s. ''Ease awes,'' guffaws the talking mule, eyes as corrective to ear's reduction of kitten's seductive vocabulary turned to ''mews'' is snot enough to lose amid typos the essence of our text beckoning assent. Anxiety of response conducts meaning to lowest denominator, prefaces foreplay plying tongue to punctuation, a setup. ''My reputation is in your mouth'' is in your mind (read aloud) allows no reading. Speak up or forever hold your piece: this is the place. Word bytes man, and the apple drops. Submit to reading. Now read this. And this. This. This.

Thus. Toss. Tsk, tsk. One gets lost. Lust accounts meter. Made my morning into song sung. Lung got it wrong, tho, stung by redaction: ink is glue. The visible flickers filtered so, selected is neglected, name of the not seen. To construct a clock imagine time seizable in units, sizeable in eunuchs, laggards playing tag to communicate past tense thought. We live in the house that Juan bought, rebuilding steps that spiral up to a meaning over my head rent with practical implication, make it nuance, shade's shift tracking sun's course, cloud muted, the mind is a terrible thing (think). To the bottom, bent pole limits parking, lottery of comprehension to any statement but convention restricts error only narrowly, stop signs vs. stars' names in the night sky, anarchy of house types in town by which to discern home in the dark become regular in the newer tracts, pattern recognition of birds in flight, a walk in the right woods. Words would do it were they real (would they were) but signifieds drain them, hemophiliac meaning, all we can speak of caged in thought insulates action, friction of syntax fought the intention, sparks connotation to belie melody, whomp bop a do bop, pink and green houses, blue glass, the old woman who lives in a shack, kettle's whistle, incomputable smear to greet ear and eye can do nothing but sort, leaving a trail that sought only to lay a track which, sounded, marked a possible present (this), activity grounded in its own proceeding, bleeding store-bought ink onto spongy page.

The abstractions of history, lethal as a foodstamp, clarify the legal real, an all-over texture, the white race to oblivion, the white rice stacked in sacks in a valley town for the displaced Laotian farmer, a frown seen is a sign of displeasure, a fond scene measures the papers' coverage, "human interest" being neither fosters purchase, sculpted tragedy of a playground killing turned into "features" fathers a false remorse (sullen competent cop shakes head), mothers no new insight, the boy just bled 2 pages away from where Garfield contemplates lasagna. Disjunct art-meaning of later collage framed against white gallery wall bends context into content, the difference it makes that the girl rising, mouth open, in horror over the student's dead body in Kent was overweight, message in the politics of appearance not lost on the applicant for what's really a sales job, degree in museum studies. Some do, however, choose education, mechanism by which to lose close connection to the culture of the "working class," whoever that was, solution to my parents' oppression being to change sides (reverse image). Perverse imagination to make equations against scale, as if to sell such small reproductions of thought: no ideas but in context. Form gathers force (my credo) for what purpose but use, source for an assault on habit. Seeming clarity inhibits thought as it ought not. Boy dead because he spoke wrong tongue. Boy George, my hero. You survive. Others. Will. Not.

Now. How. Ever. Buy futures. Bird features feathers. Beard furthers the casual look. Inverse of camouflage, open at the collar: pert. Polo shirt pink pastel backlit in the La Jolla window beside the folded tie. A small wooden box on the dresser in which her father had once kept cufflinks now held only a vial of cocaine and a tiny spoon. The diskettes were kept in what looked like a card file across from the overstuffed easy chair with its faded burgundy brocade upon which lay the sleeping ocelot like any other housepet near the window to the sea. Tennessee fireworks factory goes kerblam, fine rain of body parts, make it noise, red against blue of the news studio, cut to cued dissociation, sailboat silhouetted against vast setting sun, beer glass in foreground rising full until just the slightest foam spills over and this is the sole lamp in the cramped apartment, family of five fresh from Taiwan. Plums too small to eat have begun to drop, the fog if you look closely has its shapes and shadows, the wind in the trees is loud, I can't tell over it if that's a dog barking or the steady squeal of a saw, black beetle on a yellow leaf, parsley gone to seed and the brown cat atop the back fence sniffs the air, too cool to rain, not a fly or bee in sight, the sameness of any day against another accumulates that sadness which becomes restraint in everyone older feigning wiser, orange cat on the porch turns around and sits, such simple acts set beside each other build.

Hand-held, the image thru the pen's lens wobbles as it pans, sweep to right margin, pins sound to paper but the mind adrift hobbles after, gathering few vague echoes of intent, so tend the senses wisely or they tangle, angles frame the object hued by light, hard edged, wedged into an imagined sight but lost, the page turned, the cost of dreaming as you stare at words, birds migrating toward a punctuation, partial truths are all we get, letters home, honed, the bone of thought rings in the head, a sort of bell within a spire, what is higher than sight is heard, hurt, herds these small black beasts of graphics forth. I sit and you set the table, used it and able to do so again (you sit and I set the table, used it and able to do so again): which of us reads, which writes, or writing reads, seeds of a process which binds, not blind to the separateness of different lives, always we find strangers on the bus, but print is a bond we learned by rote, in rows, years ago. Each step taken jars the old porch, beams cracking along the grain, white spots of bird drops speckle the brown paint, the horizontals bowed and perpendiculars slanting, a few nails painted over when they should have been hammered back down. Heat-seeking, the reading eye zooms in on denotation, an old statue gone pale blue in the park with its skirt of broken bottles, dark green. The color chart fused in the eye bears arbitrary borders, blue-green, blue-gray, purple. The globe closes to a focus, or widens and blinks. Thought burdens sight by erasure. The instinct is learned. Blue iris. Brown lash. Yoke. Yolk.

But. Bit. Chewing. Down into. Onto a chunk of. Ontological chocolate. Horizontal on top of it, the sky is not flat. Venn proof by intersection of air into yard or room, such subsets of otherness. A yam what a yam, Ham's syllogism knew Yorick, Powhatten's bridge off coast of Cuba into candied doubt und so max out by the cut. Dive, he sad, for rice flakes, watch what is given (is given back), freedom's just another word, old rooms so silent of their births and deaths, brooms push dust toward a meaning, the moaning wind in the trees thought by some to be their fathers. In the desert once I heard silence, a startling thing, not wind, not even the skitter of a lizard over gravel, until the roar of blood in my head, high pitched, a clear tone, seemed about to deafen and I thought, thinking words, as if to fear a soundless world, still, stillness, knowing even motion to be but an image of time, and that but memory's projection. The idea is to inform all of their layoff at once, at the shift's end, a note on the timecard, telling each to return tomorrow for their severance plus a half-day outplacement clinic, resume skills or retraining: in 1983, the average manufacturing plant lasts just seven years and you can lease the technology out, contracting for the product, keeping capital mobile, wages down, which has its impact on poetry, that writing whose value is not that it has none, but the image presented, craft-centered, of what working could be, the care in the word.

The car in the yard: the ward healers of tenure bicker (suspending Spenser, choosing Chaucer), make it known is such a small demand, not one literate among them in the face of a single syllable sounded, soft and simple, ample enough to sample the whole of the world's thought rounded in the mouth, but curriculum demands division into genre and the vision is gone of a possible writing, sighting the opaque nameless things which fill a garden so hard to fathom, the world at random forcing form is not a farm of hardened meanings, for knowledge cannot be taught. Say that what he wrote were words, heard but never hardened into objects foreign to

POTES & POETS PRESS PUBLICATIONS

Miekal And, Book 7, Samsara Congeries
Bruce Andrews, Excommunicate
Bruce Andrews, from Shut Up
Todd Baron, dark as a hat
Lee Bartlett, Red Scare
Beau Beausoleil, in case / this way two things fell
Steve Benson, Two Works Based on Performance
Charles Bernstein, Amblyopia
Charles Bernstein, Conversation with Henry Hills
Charles Bernstein, disfrutes
Clark Coolidge, A Geology
Cid Corman, Essay on Poetry
Cid Corman, Root Song
Tina Darragh, Exposed Faces
Alan Davies, a an av es
Alan Davies, Mnemonotechnics
Alan Davies, Riot Now
Jean Day, from No Springs Trail
Ray DiPalma, New Poems
Rachel Blau DuPlessis, Tabula Rosa
Theodore Enslin, Case Book
Theodore Enslin, Meditations on Varied Grounds
Theodore Enslin, September's Bonfire
Norman Fischer, The Devices
Steven Forth, Calls This
Peter Ganick, Two Space Six
Carla Harryman, Vice
Susan Howe, Federalist 10
Janet Hunter, in the absence of alphabets
P. Inman, backbite
P. Inman, Think of One
P. Inman, waver
Jackson MacLow, Prose & Verse from the Early 80's
Barbara Moraff, Learning to Move
Janette Orr, The Balcony of Escape
Maureen Owen, Imaginary Income

Keith Rahmings, Printouts
Dan Raphael, Oops Gotta Go
Dan Raphael, The Matter What Is
Dan Raphael, Zone du Jour
Maria Richard, Secondary Image / Whisper Omega
Kit Robinson, Up Early
Laurie Schneider, Pieces of Two
James Sherry, Lazy Sonnets
Ron Silliman, B A R T
Ron Silliman, Lit
Ron Silliman, from Paradise
Pete Spence, Almanak
Pete Spence, Elaborate at the Outline
Diane Ward, Being Another / Locating in the World
Craig Watson, The Asks
Hannah Weiner, Nijole's House

Potes & Poets Press Inc
181 Edgemont Avenue
Elmwood CT 06110

their making, senses shifting but not to settle (none too subtle), taking out of talk & all that reading a bottled ship not to chase whales in but yourself until the shelf of this impulse swelled and he understood it better — say what he wrote weren't words, that he merely scripted letters. A cat is a stylized wildness chewing grass, blue inhuman eyes over which the sky fills with clouds, white scraps preceding the gray bank that pushes over the houses by the ocean, the garden damp smells stronger, a plum drops. Parrots of the past unite, for what have you to lose but that thru which you live, dream-headed, our own cages more elaborate than any. Voices in the dark, wires tangled, hark to find not an answer but an echo, barking. I know a house of mud and wattles made (no I don't). Gulls circling over the valley. It's the end of May. A hard wind. Thin sun. One. Room.

Roam. Wide. Not build. In it, "A." The el to the Loop. Lit up, writing down: balances. The boys in the binding, the buoys, discipline limits. Ears arc what's harped, I's wide, wade in the foam of, the form is a half shell (my bell), held up. Hurts harden over but are not erased, and in each case I was to what degree guilty, silly centered careless love but an indulgence. In sequins lights shine real serial, un aleph beth, garlanded sin tacks sharp consequence, flex sun's spotted circumstance all Latinate, the lit in it falls to the were, he rows to the sure lea, a lie: thus did we cross the tea. I spy: see shore, 3 masts approaching must broach a new whorl, he, he coming to z'real, breach a broken syntax teaching each a token surreal displacement of the rolling feel of it, eye's wheel, tolling signals rodeo's begun, radio's on, the sun (radiant) fills the air, what hair remains on my head is blowing, the future flowing in off the sea smells sweet. A word wide is deep also heard right, rate of exchange, sides edged by white space placed in a row go forward, knowing only where they've been as possible site to future meaning, hybrid as Marcie's white rose leaning over the fence, name's a neighbor, each a particular as against the typical, person sighted about to cross the street, city mapped in the mind is a grid, greed's a knowledge oddly used, hidden is that you I'd bid to speak with, a letter mailed at random, ladder to the wall's top (edge of the paper) that stops pretending the vision's beyond, left there, mark of an old desire.